T0194854

# Dove Love

A Collection of Poems

By Carolyn Burroughs Dixon

WESTBOW
P R E S S®
A DIVISION OF THOMAS NELSON
& ZONDERVAN

This book is a work of non-fiction. Unless otherwise noted, the author and the publisher make no explicit guarantees as to the accuracy of the information contained in this book and in some cases, names of people and places have been altered to protect their privacy. WestBow Press books may be ordered through booksellers or by contacting:

WestBow Press
A Division of Thomas Nelson & Zondervan
1663 Liberty Drive
Bloomington, IN 47403
www.westbowpress.com
1 (866) 928-1240

Because of the dynamic nature of the Internet, any web addresses or links contained in this book may have changed since publication and may no longer be valid. The views expressed in this work are solely those of the author and do not necessarily reflect the views of the publisher, and the publisher hereby disclaims any responsibility for them.

Any people depicted in stock imagery provided by Getty Images are models, and such images are being used for illustrative purposes only. Certain stock imagery © Getty Images.

All Scripture quotations, unless otherwise indicated, are taken from the Holy Bible, New International Version®, NIV®. Copyright ©1973, 1978, 1984, 2011 by Biblica, Inc.™ Used by permission of Zondervan. All rights reserved worldwide. www.zondervan.comThe "NIV" and "New International Version" are trademarks registered in the United States Patent and Trademark Office by Biblica, Inc.™

Scripture marked (KJV) is taken from the King James Version of the Bible.

ISBN: 978-1-9736-7217-3 (sc)
ISBN: 978-1-9736-7216-6 (hc)
ISBN: 978-1-9736-7218-0 (e)

Library of Congress Control Number: 2019911783

Print information available on the last page.

WestBow Press rev. date: 08/13/2019

# Resident Dove

Listen, the dawn comes, and I think I hear
That resident dove cooing in my ear
A comforting sound reminds me of love
Could be he has a message from above
Quiet morning, soothing familiar sound
Sunlight glows on that rose-mauve chest so round
Gathering angels with fluttering wings
White dove foreshadows joy of glory sings
Come, Holy Spirit perch at my window
Bringing His presence and let the wind blow
Dove of Peace is waiting with loving care
Holding onto faith until we get there

**"I saw the Spirit come down from
heaven as a dove..." John 1:32**

# Waving Palm Fronds

The people cheered
He was revered
Riding that lowly beast
They spread robes, praised, these least
Unseen kingdom and their high priest
Triumphal entry, start the feast
God and tradition to exalt
Too quickly turning point to fault
Jesus chose to do
Changed everything they knew
Taught six days more
Wept for them sore
Wonder what I would say
Had I been there that day
Waving palm fronds lifting "All hail!"
Witnessed the kiss of betrayal
Heard His agony of the flail
No hand could rend the temple veil

As He hung on that tree
Where He suffered for me
Hail Chosen One
Beloved Son

**"He is not here; He has risen!" Luke 24:6**

# BC JC AD

So different before He came
They told the priest of their shame
Endless rituals it seemed
Buy the doves and be redeemed
Animal's blood would atone
Daily grinding, pressing stone
Harvested crops, planted seed
Unaware of spirit's need
Old Testament

So different after He came
While on earth, He took my shame
Jesus, moment The Light beamed
Sacrificed once, Lamb redeemed
His blood only will atone
Temples built on Cornerstone
Nations re-born from one seed
Praise and worship, Spirit-freed
New Testament

# Call Out, Reach Out

That's right! Call His name, Lord! Out loud!
No fear, no division allowed
He chose us; let Him keep leading
Quickly pray, hasten speed-reading
Write down what He says when you meet
Share love, pray with joy, those you greet
They need Him, they know who He is
But they don't know they can be His
Feed body and soul; give His love
Life-giving words, fulfilled above
He's silent? Hey! God's got knee mail!
You make contact; system won't fail
Promised He would leave us never
Soon we'll be with Him forever

**'Call to me and I will answer you and tell you great and unsearchable things you do not know.' Jeremiah 33:3**

# I Give You My Heart

I give you my heart
My life every part
You gave Your life to atone
To save me; You died alone
I take a step toward Your call of love
Accepting Your plan to live above
The Only One God raised, now You're living free
The One I believe will soon return for me
Fire, wind, water, now spirit brothers
Hearts agree, nations telling others
Beauty's flower, all I will give
Received gift, for You I live
All You gave, the start
I give You my heart

**For it is with your heart that you believe and
are justified and it is with your mouth that you
confess and are saved. Romans 10:10**

# Draw the Line

He drew a line in the sand
Concession by His own hand
Accusers, cast the first stone
One by one; left them alone
The forgiven and the Pawn
In the earth the plumb was drawn
Judgment shifted by the sign
Made the cross over the line
He said, "Go and sin no more"
ENTER sign above the Door
Look for Warrior, Blood and Dove
All symbolic of His love

**Neither do I condemn you… John 8:11**

# The Light

That star in the east pointing to the Light
New life exchanged for many souls to right
He is Beauty, Light of understanding
He waits gently, listening, undemanding
Love's silence quickens, all we need to know
Warm precious moments, basking in His glow
Shut out sounds of the crescendo of might
Nothing else matters, look toward the Light
Visions of a jeweled city someday
Above all needs, nothing to block the way
Twinkling stars, walls of gems, protected site
Surrounded by Him, living in The Light

**For you were once darkness, but now you
are light in the Lord. Ephesians 5:8**

# Heart's Share

Flow from deep in my heart of hearts
Stow your love in its secret parts
Blow away harmful inward darts
Tow out the junk by loaded carts
Oh, praise His name He knows my name
No former self, I'm not the same
Owe all to Him who took the blame
Go and tell them God said He came
Slow anger, peace and silent fame
Crow resurrection! End of shame
So, you see, sometimes life's not fair
Show other children He does care
Pro Life for you, knows every hair
Row upstream through those storms we bear
Grow faith, give and have more to share
Know Him before we get up there

**In him our hearts rejoice, for we trust
in his holy name. Psalm 33:21**

# Jesus, My Darling

He says, my Darling, my Life
Cherished pet name for a wife
Don't listen some will mock it
Sealed forever heart's locket
Won't consider self or grieve
Trusting You will never leave
Jesus, jealous of my time
Closer still You are my Rhyme
Saved my soul, sin appalling
Soon I will hear You calling
Meantime I will occupy
Provision in vast supply
We're still loving and living
More receiving than giving
Listening with breath abating
Word power promise waiting

**Rescue my life from their ravages, my precious life
[my darling] from these lions. Psalm 35:17**

# Speak To Me

Speak to me, Lord, sin it would seem
Increasing threats to rule our land
Quaking, shaking us from our dream
Future promised at your right hand
Who will listen and who will hear?
Reaching up to unload their cares
Beyond the news, beyond the fear
Turning everything into prayers
Speak to me, Lord, that I may know
That voice, Your presence even now
Trading moments, I love You so
Receive me, as I humbly bow
Trusting You brought me to this place
Butterfly joy, spirit renew
Lovingly freed by Your sweet grace
Worshipping and waiting for You
To speak to me

**"…he will guide you into all truth…and he will
tell you what is yet to come." Luke 16:13**

# Songs in the Night

Merciful God in heaven above
How can I tell of your marvelous love?
Perhaps in the sound of the mourning dove
Saying, Come love, love, love.
The sweetest sounds like I've never known
Since the Holy Spirit came, spoke to me alone
What instrument is that? What note, what tone?
I hear laughter and joy, I feel at home.
Time means nothing to me anymore
Show me the colors, I want to see more
The most beautiful colors I've ever seen
Golden rainbow, effervescence, gossamer sheen.
Sweet words seem to come from everywhere
Hear them and taste them, no burdens, no care
Don't rush them, don't miss them, just be aware,
Now to His presence, He's taking me there.
Waves and waves of sweetness flood over me
Jesus has spoken and now I am free!
His love in my spirit is there to see
Oh, yes, this is a special place to be.

**...you will fill me with joy
in your presence... Psalm 16:11**

# Soaring with My Dove

He set me free; I'm free indeed
And He's the only One I need
He said it, so
I must let go
Nor more guilt from anything past
He exposed lies; I'm free at last
Listen, said He
You've been set free
The Father saw that it was good
All those sins are under the blood
Free as a bird
My spirit heard
Once again purity inside
He said He sees me as a bride
Freedom to say
Joy from today
In light of His presence I see
I believe He is Peace in me

**...they will soar on wings like eagles... Isaiah 40:31**

# Heartful

Beating…. continues to feel
Supernatural most real
Life will never be the same
Epic sagas in a name
Agape friendship is pure
Heavenly support faith sure
Undeniably present
So delightfully pleasant
Holy Spirit Sweet Treasure
Favored, loved without measure
Redeemed the time, won the bid
Captured my heart, yes You did
Now, You hold it in Your hand
Introduce the angel band
Our time has come to attend
Heaven's banquet without end

**…you believe in him and are filled with an
inexpressible and glorious joy. 1 Peter 1:8**

# For Me

It was foretold
In days of old
You came to earth
By virgin birth
For me?

The One who sent You
Is our Father too
To those who would hear
You spoke of Him here
For me.

You went about preaching
Gospel You were teaching
You were God's gift to men
You were sacrificed then
For me.

I heard You call my name
My life was never the same
And though my youth was misspent
Redeeming gift was still meant
For me!

I am the church, protected bride
Holy Spirit walks by my side
Until the day for which I yearn
I'll see your face and you'll return
For me!

**And so we will be with the Lord
forever. I Thessalonians 4:17**

## Jordan Riverboat Ride

Looks like an easy journey, tell you why,
Floating hologram perceptions . . . oh, my!
Swiftly over heaven's bridge I could fly,
Over the Jordan I see in the sky,
Stepping clouds across waters of blue,
No longer earthbound, move into the view,
On wings of faith unlimited breakthrough,
Trumpets, garden sights and music all new.
Resident congregation dressed in white,
Willingly surrounded by Him, The Light,
Suddenly, all overwhelmed by insight,
Beautiful dream; now instant return flight.
Must have patience preparing, mustn't we?
For now, soft view made to order for me,
Sky-blue-pink with a yellow border, see?
Sunset colors whisper 'time to. . .just. . .be.'

**...you shall see heaven open. John 1:51**

# The Lord your God

Joined in spirit, eyes never dim
And keep thee only unto Him
Jesus, the One who died for you
Now lives, now builds, give Him His due
Guard your heart, don't roam far and wide
Stay under His banner, abide
You belong to God's only Son
Temptation passes, glitter's gone
Pure heart, eternal life goes on
Value His love, not every whim
And keep thee only unto Him

**For your Maker is your husband- the Lord
Almighty is his name. Isaiah 54:5**

# Dove's Eyes

When You look at me with dove's eyes
I see flights home to peaceful skies
Waiting best
Building nest
Those soft black eyes, perfect roundness
Sure commitment, loving soundness
Prepare all
Then come call
Round, gray-pink-mauve like the morning
Or soft white feathers adorning
Wings flutter
Hearts mutter
I hear Your voice, the sound of cooing
Come love, love, love, Spirit wooing
Soft nuzzle
Life puzzle
Proud chest swelled, touch like a feather
Come, let us whisper together
Forever
And ever

Heartbeats at recognizing part
Each meeting reminds of the start
Two nesters
Now vespers

**How beautiful you are, my darling!…Your eyes
behind your veil are doves. Song of Songs 4:1**

## Love Thereof Turtledove

When you whisper to me sweetly
My heart follows You completely
You lead me like Zion's daughters
By dream's place of quiet waters
Overheard love's bliss in songbirds
Saw the kiss of cooing lovebirds
Your redeemed bride's embrace, therefore
I'll see His fair face through the Door
Whosoever declares affection
Receives Your Grace and Love's perfection
Heirs to sumptuous twelve-pearls measure
Glorious sapphire, glass-gold treasure
Emerald, topaz, amethyst rare
Single-pearl gate, robe and crown to wear
The marriage supper; all plans complete
Bride and Bridegroom will meet and retreat
Father's blessings, mansions waiting there
All love and worship in His wedding prayer
Kiss the nail-scarred hands, fingers interlace
Heaven's music; finishers of the race
Sweet love beyond moonbeams, forevermore
Understanding Your love more than before

A moment like that, nothing can compare
Until perfection, the Bride must prepare
I love You so, my precious King
You know me, You know everything
Bathed in Your Spirit, sing Your praise
Waiting. . .. worship a few more days
Know Your voice; hear Your words so sweet
I bow when face to face we meet
My heart is full and my joyful tears
Anticipate just a few more years
O, please, call my name, my First True Love
And kiss me again, my Turtledove
Flower of heaven, fragrance so sweet
Invited in, You reserved my seat
Obedience to The Holy One
To reign beside You, His Only Son

**I saw the Holy City, the new Jerusalem…with every
kind of precious stone. Revelation 21:2, 19**

# The Father of the Bride

O, the fierce protector of the Bride
He so wants to keep her by His side
She's been waiting for Him so long
Heart sounds between them such a sweet song
Dependent upon Him from the start
Each day an imprint upon her heart
Knowing the Father's unconditional love
That same love bestowed upon His Dove
Trusting in the Father's loving Word
By faith knowing what her spirit heard
She can turn now and trust another
With the same spirit of our Brother
Behold, The Bridegroom is the Bright Light
Welcoming His Bride dressed in pure white
The banqueting table is all set
They planned for this since the day they met
We'll walk together down streets of gold
Greatest wedding story ever told
We'll meet with the Father of the Bride
And ever live with Him side by side

**'Here's the bridegroom! Come out to
meet him!' Matthew 25:6**

# Wedding Feast

Roses, pearls and lace, diamonds endure
Relationship with Jesus secure
Purifying ways
For the coming days
That perfume drifts through my soul so sweet
Ribbon-tied thumbs, satin at my feet
Bread and cup, all forgiven
We are all dressed in linen
Today our bands
Join Holy Lands
Banqueting table is set to dine
Crystal clear goblets hold sparkling wine
Our Bridegroom the Dove
Hearts swelling with love
The Bride made ready from days of old
Mansion set…eternity threshold!

**For the wedding of the Lamb has come, and his
bride has made herself ready. Revelation 19:7**

# *Private Honor, King's Request*

Intimacy is my need
The veil is removed, my King
I, too, am Abraham's seed
Your Light revealed everything
Mingled blood covenant made
Your spoken word my cover
All future plans aside bade
Chambers hide me, soul lover
Talking finished, mouth-to-mouth kisses
No separation, removed linen
Waiting your presence, my heart misses
Encircling, enfolding, press in then
Heart is open, love revealed
Knowing, no shadow of doubt
Union agreement kiss sealed
Music floats, all else shut out
Whispered thought turned to matched sighs
Plan carried out, married then
Home – New Jerusalem skies
Renewed, we'll worship again

**Who is this King of glory? The Lord
strong and mighty... Psalm 24:8**

# The Apple of His Eye

Tell you how God loves you; please let me try
You're His precious apple, close as His eye
Much more than romantic love with a sigh
He knows me; I'm as close as His eye
He understands, unlike men, He can't lie
He forgives us, we forgive them, that's why
It's not enough, is it?...to just get by
Along with Jesus, the old self must die
He arose, He arose, now free am I
I know He hears and answers, I'll soon fly
By faith, ride His chariot to the sky
Sing over me Spirit, let's soar on high
One day soon, eternity ribbons tie
Now I keep that vision in my mind's eye
I hear Your Word's apples, come and draw nigh
Protect me as the daughter of Your eye

**Keep me as the apple of your eye... Psalm 17:8**

# Every Woman's Dream

O Where is my love, did I hear his voice?
I'm holding my breath 'til he makes his choice.
I have never met a man quite like you,
It's the man you are, more than things you do.
Whatever happens, and from here on out,
My faith in love is what it's all about.
You're not like the rest, no need to compare,
You're sensitive and loving, and you care,
A man of integrity, not too proud,
To give of himself, enough time allowed,
To talk and listen and hear me well,
This growing closeness, valued truth to tell.
We met at church, where women wait to find
A man who will be sensitive and kind,
Strong and mature, not ruled by emotion,
Firm and established in God's devotion.
I believe in love, it won't go away;
We'll be together in heaven someday.

**Many waters cannot quench love, rivers
cannot wash it away. Song of Songs 8:7**

# Women Who Wait

Young women wait for their first date
From men who want to stay out late
Young women, study; plan your lives
Just wait, at least until he drives
Women who wait to be a bride
Keep a man waiting by her side
Women who wait for the right man
He's worth the wait, they know they can
Brides wait count down to wedding day
Waited on Him; their vows they'd say
Brides wait doctor's signaled due date
Family now - baby, you and mate
Women who wait like their mothers
For children who leave their covers
Women who wait to take their turn
Careers, hidden talents, they learn
Grandmothers wait, babies; numbers
Sifting mem'ries while she slumbers
Grandmothers wait new beginnings
Seasons of love, heaven's winnings

**Blessed is she who has believed that what the Lord has said to her will be accomplished. Luke 1:45**

# Anticipation

What is this music in my ears?
Soothing and calming all my fears
I'm only sure of just one thing
It won't be denied, this feeling
Bubbling over, wants to speak out
Unconditional, there's no doubt
Things sound different, look different too
O, what am I going to do?
Softly, softly, whisper my name
Please tell me this isn't a game
My life will never be the same
Fragmented and head is to blame.
Face set like flint, never moving
Grounded and no need for proving
Love waits but never demanding
Heart is rushing, chest expanding.
Freely given, received or not
Again, it covers every blot.
Love's hope of heart is not so wise
Hear me out, remove your disguise
Prayers and blessings at your side

Happy should you make me your bride.
Waiting is not painful, my love
Hoping keeps love alive, my dove
Love is strong, true bond marathon
Till hope of heaven, love lives on.

**...as you eagerly wait for our Lord Jesus
Christ to be revealed. 1 Corinthians 1:7**

# Wedding Blessing

Emotional rivers deep
They have promises to keep
And treasured wisdom to reap
Today our hearts also leap
Expectation
Communication
Christ as Leader will install
Admiration above all
Joy abound and faith recall
Honor loving duty call
Jubilation
Celebration
Dotted line, circle of two
Hopeful day, shiny and new
Lighted pathway, focused view
God's great blessings over you

**...Blessed are those who are invited to the
marriage supper of the Lamb. Revelation 19:9**

# *His and Hers*

Husband and wife
Circle of life
Learning of His Word
Children will be heard
Remembered family jokes
Carried further by their folks
Treasured and precious times are these now
Recreation with them each allow
Teaching them what my Father taught me
Pray and trust in God, then peace they'll see
Enjoy them now and don't wait
As parents, you'll both be great
Hard work worth the call
Jesus loves you all
Happy for you
All my love, too

**Her husband has full confidence in her. Proverbs 31:11**

# Marriage

It's not fifty, but one hundred percent
O, God, I don't know this person you sent
Or did You? I don't know why he went
I thought those vows were something we both meant
It's like a third person you care about
Like the Holy Spirit, no room for doubt
Marriage aims inward and doesn't want out
Circle of love sealed; a visible shout
Once agreed upon, love won't go away
But is it enough to make us both stay?
Words are like jewels, some fall where they may
Commitment has power and finds a way
Like friends and giving, it drives what we owe
Pride topples after weaving to and fro
I'm helpless if you decide you must go
Love will still be there; some things you just know
Like tempered steel, stronger for the blending
Forgiveness is key, together bending
Stay together, strong signals we're sending
I love you with God's love that's unending

**-guard it with the help
of the Holy Spirit…2 Timothy 1:13**

# Beautiful Secret

What is this flutter near this heart of mine?
Like the tug-tug-tug on a fishing line.
My secret, I can't stop smiling inside,
Very soon I won't be able to hide.
It grows inside me as a sign of life,
All-knowing, pondering, mother and wife.
Yes, it's love and much more, it goes beyond,
The simple, established, two-person bond.
Now I'm linked with all those who've gone before,
We all know the secret forevermore.
Love made it possible to live to be,
In this moment and it comes down to me.
Isn't the body an amazing thing?
The picture of life can move me to sing.
Hello, little baby; look at that smile,
Let's take a trip together, stay awhile.
Suddenly a family, nothing said,
New Mom and Dad's eyes meet over your head.

**...the time came for the baby to be born. Luke 2:6**

# Make Good Memories

Life is so precious; precious worth
Loving care surrounding your birth
Learning to talk
Anxious to walk
He's your father
'Twas no bother
Remember love
THAT you're sure of
Hear me tell you
Of your value
Sensitive to other ages
Stronger when tragedy rages
Know it will come
So, don't play dumb
When you're older
Life is colder
It's not all bad
Look what you've had
Peaches and cream
A lovely dream

Make good memories, my young one
While you're learning and having fun
Faith and love; tremendous amount
Obey the keys; go make it count

**God gave Solomon wisdom and great insight 1 Kings 4:29**

# Male Pride

That peacock, strutting around,
with his chest swelled,
shaking his feathers
and doing a dance
in front of your face.
He dances away those fears
and takes dominion
over his kingdom. God has made him
well able to protect your nest.
Oh, let him strut in all his beauty,
continue to admire his feathers
and the palace remains a happy place.
Your quiet beauty and dignity,
little bird, are his peace, rest.
Proud of you, he conquers
enemies of the heart
and they leave without a trace.
Let him have the last word
of authority given to him.
Cover his mistakes with your
thoughtful acts of love,
a smile and a little grace.

**David reigned over all Israel, 1 Chronicles 18:14**

# Misunderstanding

A little tiny thing
Became a great big thing
I lost it, I lost it
Got myself in a snit
Suddenly it got loud
Certainly can't be proud
Like a hot air balloon
Pressure seemed to boom
Words are everywhere
Hanging, floating out there
The clock strikes double twelves
We must forgive ourselves
No need for one more tear
Forgotten by next year
Already in the past
Now I can sleep at last

**Forgiving each other just as in Christ
God forgave you. Ephesians 4:32**

## Run To Love

Run to him chosen, don't run away
Love him and pray for him ev'ry day
Give him private time to work his plan
He sees your love and feels like a man
Tell him you need him and go his way
Listen and learn from all he might say
Believe in him and give him your all
You will know joy, oh!…see him stand tall
Run to her, see her, watching your eyes
Your face a sign, she whispers and sighs
If she cries, will you ignore her tears?
Believe me, your words will calm her fears
Yes, she loved you way back then
Say the words she needs to hear again
Giving is blessing, you know it's true
Love her, she'll do anything for you
Run to Him, make it a daily thing
With the best gifts that you both can bring
Don't relive the past, what's done is done
God gives His blessing – you love His Son

Sure of teaching as listening hearts could
Together you'll be everything good
Yes, He saw your eyes, He heard your prayer
Always loved you, He's waiting up there

**But the greatest of these is love 1 Corinthians 13:13**

# Cater To Guests

Invite them in say, "Have a seat"
"Sit down and let me wash your feet"
A little this; a little that
Fatness in your soul, your place mat
Taste and see that the Lord is good
Then go tell the whole neighborhood
She looked back; it wasn't his fault
Dried up like a pillar of salt
Like the Dead Sea, too much flavor
Better a sweet-smelling savor
Parables of life-giving bread
Taste like honey, His words in red
Then the cup. . .. or. . .. milk of kindness
His Son's light will heal our blindness
We savored the King's spicy meat
He paid the price and it's His treat
Manna digested; satisfied
His faithfulness is verified
Fruit of peace and gifts honey-sweet
Banquet blessings when next we meet

**'Go out to the roads and country lanes
and make them come in, so that my
house will be full.' Luke 14:23**

# Who Cares?

Doesn't matter anyway
Things'll never change
I could change my mind today
Give myself full range
What would be the point of that?
If only things were changed
Looked at things from where I sat
All were rearranged
Others would remain the same
I can just see that
Taking credit giving blame
Wiping feet on mat
Just relax, it'll be fun
Take it easy, Dear
Who will listen? Only One
He is always near
Even bad days are brighter
Seen with new insight
Every shared burden lighter
Look toward the Light

 **Cast all your anxiety on him because
he cares for you. I Peter 5:7**

# You're Never Alone

Sometimes love is not enough?
Girl, I know you had it rough
Take it light and take it slow
Love won't go away, you know
Look in the mirror, what do you see?
You're still alive, aren't you? Look at me!
Disaster reports, talk show reviews
You know you can't stand no more bad news
Screen crawl warning – disconnect
Bible verses recollect
You'll find love there if you would
Rockin' chair sure does look good
Music in your soul, hear it? I can!
I'm tellin' you, I know one good Man
When it seems like all your friends left town
The Carpenter's love won't let you down

**"...Never will I leave you; never will I
forsake you..." Hebrews 13:5**

# High Valued Pearls

What, Girl?
What, Pearl?
What are you talking about?
You are not a knockabout
You'll be a Christian throughout
Yes, I'm sure, I have no doubt
Though to my cost
Detoured, got lost
Stomped on by those pigs in mud
Hidden beauty wisdom's bud
Yeah, mud got on me, that's mean
But my soul can be washed clean
Though deeds were real
It's the same deal
You think no hope, alone, but
Identity died, so what?
Your spirit's not dead, so fly
Hope's alive! Unlimited sky!
Never mind those
Mud grows a rose

Purified by Blood; made white
He'll protect us; not by might
Cultured by Spirit; God's girls
We are His high-valued pearls

**"…the kingdom of heaven is like a merchant
looking for fine pearls." Matthew 13:45**

# Who's my Neighbor?

She used to live down the street before she moved
Once-in-a-while we'd meet; I felt behooved
We'd talk on the phone
Our secrets, our own
I sure miss that now, you know?
Remember when…?
Where is she, where did she go?
Let's see, that's been…
Talked to her Father
He said no bother
We'll all be together free, and she'll be there
My Father lives next to me; He heard my prayer
Asked Him about you
You're my neighbor, too
That's not all you need, is it? What can I do?
Coming soon and we'll visit…Have gifts for you
Until then, let's pray
You could move today…

**'Love your neighbor as yourself.' Luke 10:27**

# This Place

This place on the map; just one dot
The world in one moment, but how?
Some are praying, some, maybe not
Can we gather together now?
This place where I live, familiar
The children's laughter is now gone
Our mature views are similar
Some of our mem'ries will live on
This place in my life comes with pain
And some things, some turns just went wrong
I'll be back on my feet again
Let me hear a holiday song
This place in my heart looks refreshed
Swept clean and the cracks all mended
Words of love and peace inter-meshed
Every prayer and need attended
This place we're going, made of gems
New Jerusalem spirits raised
Instruments! Shouts! Choirs and Anthems!
King of Kings! Let our Lord be praised!

**...the Holy City, Jerusalem, coming down out
of heaven from God. Revelation 21:10**

# You and Me and Them

Do you love me beyond just what you see?
Would you change this or that, what I could be?
Read the past in these lines, you'll know me well
I've been tempted, sinned, heard whispers from hell
Troubles just like you, sure you get the gist
Want prayers answered now from my selfish list
What you get's not what you see
And God has helped even me
Here we go again but you just don't know
What I've been through, from here where do I go?
The best place Holy Spirit and in prayer
Talk to God, read His Word, find answers there
More than money, beauty, health gourmet meal
Eternal life, rhema words, help that's real
When you don't know what to do
Yes, God can help even you
What about all those others without sight?
More and more what they're doing is not right
They have strange beliefs and they talk funny
Get away with all and have more money

You and me we're okay, that's what He'll say
Tell those in the dark wait not one more day
What's more, beyond the problem
Is, God will help even them

**For by grace are you saved by faith; Ephesians 2:8**

# Best Friend

Today I had a talk with my best friend
I told her my patience was near the end
She's known me since we were very young
She listened, had ideas, among
Other things you could do is write a book
Everything's gonna be okay, just look
At all the things we've come through okay
And tomorrow is another day
East coast, Southwest, hot, cold and back again
Hurricanes, tornadoes, children and men
Who loved us then, went by in a blur
Through it all, my best friend is still her
Tonight, I had a talk with Our Best Friend
I know He'll be with us beyond the end
He knew us before we were babies
We hear yes and amen, not maybes
He took everything for us on His back
His great love for us, y'all, is never slack
They wrote a book with all He's been through
Words in red tell what we say and do

He'll come back one day, and this life will cease
To be, and with Him forever increase
O, my faith, hang on until the end
Soon we'll all see Jesus, Our Best Friend

**...a friend who sticks closer than a brother. Proverbs 18:24**

# Prayer

Have we forgotten how to pray?
What will work, when, or what to say?
Still, repetition is okay
Speaking the Word out loud each day
For answers it is the best way
Can you pray for me? Yes, you may
You know you should pray every day
What? With all I've been through? No way!
Heart confessions will friends betray?
What Happened? What happened? We say
Go to the doctor yesterday?
Maybe he can make it okay
I'll pray if I have time today
Or maybe God will make a way
Like children we whine and we bray
Is He in a good mood today?
Get what you give, I heard them say
Lord, you love us, give us our way
Keep all unpleasantness at bay
Heal, save, and prosper us we pray

Praise drives evil spirits away
We've had milk, give us meat today
Repentance, forgiveness in fray
Show us Your blessings soon, okay?
Lead us, guide us, don't let us stray
Protection, favor every day
Wait on Him, fruit served on His tray
Intercession, power to sway
Agreement, faith punch words we say
Spirit to God through Jesus pray
Thank You God for the Son's light ray
Pearls and gems at His feet we'll lay
Plead cities and worlds turn His way
Mature, ready, soon-coming day
Check lamps, mount up, shed feet of clay
Promise kept, it could be today

**Be joyful in hope, patient in affliction,
faithful in prayer. Romans 12:12**

# One Shoe on the Highway

A terrible accident…HURRY!…No time to cry,
(Yes, she has one shoe) …We need you to identify…
We're doing everything we can…Please, don't cry.
It doesn't look good, she may die…What?…Why?
Where's the faith to bring her back…That's my kid!
I prayed You'd snatch her from evil and You did!
Police report, "No seat belt" the final clue.
Oh…here…is this her other shoe?
What am I gonna do?
With just one shoe?
One shoe on the highway,
O, God, be merciful to me today.
Well, Sweetie, they can't hurt you now, go ahead and cry.
Oh, no…a siren, doesn't matter, don't need to know why.
Angels took her to heaven, How do I know?
Because God made a covenant and that makes it so.
Someday I'll find her the other side of the sky,
Someday soon…with the last sigh
I know what we'll do
We'll try on shoes, a thousand pair or two!

Come on now, you've gotta be strong,
Do I? Am I really? For how long?
Oh, Jesus, I can't; I don't want to be strong,
It's too quiet, something is very wrong.
Would have been twenty-five, she can't make it today,
She's gone, not far, but she's gone away.
It's been almost a year since that terrible day,
The last thing she said, "Mom, it's gonna be okay."
Can't look now, can't keep one shoe, but I can strive,
Through pictures and talking, keep mem'ries alive.
It was an accident, we all have to die,
Grief stages; you may see me have a good cry.
There's a flower in heaven from a beautiful seed,
I look forward with joy to our reunion indeed.
She's up there decorating our place I bet,
The flowers, the colors, the jokes, don't forget.
I'll be there someday soon, but not now,
I've got to get through this…somehow,
Give me a minute…I'll think of something.
How I've missed her…but I know one thing,
A mother's prayers will help us to bear,
What remains ahead 'til we get there.
Another accident, yes, I knew
Today on the highway…just one shoe.

**"…but I will see you again and you**
**will rejoice…" John 16:22**

55

# Children in Heaven

Sometime later if not today
Lord, bring us the right words to say
Don't take on any of the guilt
Think of the Rock on which you're built
Yes, part of you dies everyday
You'll see God's heart in a new way
He means what He says in His word
You'll remember something you heard
Bruises won't show, don't stop running
Time for living, chance for sunning
Rock back and forth and hold on tight
Let Him help you get through the night
Soon you'll begin again to feel
Promised joy in the Spirit seal
Meet our children in heaven, too
In the meantime, we'll pray for you

**The promise is for you and your children… Acts 2:39**

# To Parents Left Behind

We didn't meet your children, but our children did
They greeted them in heaven, yes I'm sure they did
And yet we miss them here
And yet we miss them here
Sometimes our kids run into a wall of trouble
But God said that in this world there would be trouble
Oh, hear us cry at night
Oh, hear us cry at night
See the flowers, read the words, we'll do what we can
Life among the living, by faith I know we can
Pray some will hear the call
Pray some will hear the call
We'll meet in heaven one day soon, we know we will
God still answers prayers and questions, He said He will
And you'll want to be there
And you'll want to be there

**...together with them in the clouds to meet
the Lord in the air. 1 Thessalonians 4:17**

# Little White Cross

Little white cross
Signifying loss
In the middle of the highway
I wonder what happened that day?
There was someone else in the car
Yes, but O, now you can see far!
The cross is still there in that place
You were here, then gone from the race.
Never forget
It is there yet
As a reminder of that day
You are gone but not far away.
Another wooden cross is gone
But the life given there lives on.
See His hands and feet? Hear His heart?
You've been together from the start.
No, there's no loss
White cross, wooden cross.

**"…It is finished…" John 19:30**

# $S$orrow

After the lovely funeral tribute agreed home-going joys,
Through the motions, belongings distribute, wry humor
and new toys? After sickening sweet smell of flowers
oh, please, what will I do? Reminders, long, silent,
empty hours my one thought; I miss you. Shock, denial,
anger, guilt, acceptance sometimes all in one day, Only
forgiveness, acts of repentance will bind life words we say.
I'll just have to find a hollering road; music carries me
through, Books, time, fam'ly and friends to share the
load; faith in Him I talk to. We're not held in the
clutches of sorrow blinded, deceived, helpless, God's
plan, His Son, the Hope of tomorrow obedience will bless.
I know the Man of Sorrows died alone and I may do
the same, It was for our sins He chose to atone
Oh, praise His Holy name!

**...Jesus is the Christ, the Son of God, and that by
believing you may have life in his name. John 20:31**

59

# Missing You

A sound in the morning dew
I sent the geese down to you
Season of change makes me sad
Losing leaves and plans I had
Vivid color burns and falls
Indoor decoration calls
Cooking, tea, happy and warm
Pan in hand, ideas swarm
Reach by paper? Wrote your name
News to tell you much the same
I'd rather hear what you say
On this sunny, crisp fall day
Change coming, it's in the air
Wait and listen, I'll be there
Each one the other misses
There'll be more hugs and kisses

**...we wait for it patiently. Romans 8:25**

# Recovery

Shock, denial, anger, acceptance, guilt
Say not the five on which my house is built
Stages not denied but heed the warning
They're gone and soon we must turn from mourning
Lord, Come sit with us while we pray
Help us to see the light of day
We need to catch our breath
We've all been hit by death
Your words taste of sweetness
We will learn Your meekness
Old things are gone and passed away
Surely it's gonna be okay
Yes, we will still miss them once in a while
Memories, a few tears, through them we smile
Turning faces to God in these last years
Our bright hope the day there'll be no more tears

**...though I walk through the valley of the shadow of death,
I will fear no evil, for you are with me... Psalm 23:4**

# Angels Our Warriors

I understand there are angels out there.
Are they young women with beautiful hair?
We all want angels given to our care,
They must be strong and big enough to square.
The Bible tells us they are big, strong men,
Who told them "Fear not" again and again,
Messengers, guards, rollers of stones, swordsmen,
The same God-given power now as then.
Send comforting warriors; cupids won't do,
When it comes to protecting me or you,
Those who serve God in heaven and earth, too.
Won't it be great when we get to heaven?
It won't be long, though we don't know just when;
We must speak to children, women and men,
Speaking God's Word about angels 'til then.

**Are not all angels ministering spirits sent to serve
those who will inherit salvation? Hebrews 1:14**

# R. I. P.

My future will be
Just imagine we
Together will be
So just look for me
You first under there
Life is so unfair
Our usual care
We've nothing to wear
So, under the trees
Let us take our ease
Ah, cool summer breeze
Next stop heaven please
Rest In Peace
Rip off the cover
By faith I'll hover
Green fields of clover
This time is over
Limits forget it
Bring along your wit
Your new robe will fit
Every song's a hit

Come on rise and shine
Prayers from nine to nine
Rest in faith is mine
Peace to thine and thine
Rise In Power

**"...and the dead in Christ will rise
first." 1 Thessalonians 4:16**

# Rise to New Life

Is all death punishment and losing?
Life on earth is not of our choosing
Eternal life is the crown jewel
And love transforms into renewal
We wanted them to live forever
Healthy, happy days; changing never
While the grieving tend the grave
Stumbling children misbehave
Producers of anger led by strife
Cities without trees, water or life
Wake up while you can come to yourself
Put mourning and anger on the shelf
Read something to them from the Good Book
Change their minds about the way things look
Breathe the precious life He gives
Everywhere His Spirit lives

**"...he has crossed over from death to life." John 5:24**

# The Patience Room

It could have been worse
Thank God for my nurse
Angels of mercy day and night
Everything okay? Feel all right?
Round-the-clock care, a clean, stenciled room
No fear, worry, examples of doom
Just let me rest
I'll give my best
Wounded to the hilt
Bruised by swords of guilt
Only presented with this day
Looked for humor along the way
Thank you my friend, for sharing the load
Feelings, circumstances on this road
I'll be okay
He's in today

**"This is my body given for you…"**
**"This cup is the new covenant in my blood,**
**which is poured out for you." Luke 22:19,20**

# Night Worry

Help me! I don't know what to do!
I'm trying to keep my mind on You
Blessings and peace have come before
Can't think why I'd ask for more...
Feel like I'm standing on the brink
Another adjustment? Can't think!
They're all fine from what I can see
What would they think if they knew me?
I'm inside here and there's no sound
Help me get back on solid ground
Heavy emotions running deep
All prayers to You for I must sleep

**If you continue in your faith, established
and firm... Colossians 1:23**

# *It's All Temporary*

It's all temporary, this pain
Recognized it wafting again
Unseen except in that nightmare
Did I miss angels unaware?
It's all temporary, feelings…
Woke up, stopped staring at ceilings
Cleaned the temple and moved around
Basic faith and joy still abound
It's all temporary-------hurry!
Settle accounts and don't worry
Remedy: commitment to prayers
You made it through, Jesus still cares
It's all temporary, on earth
Endurance, character shows worth
Trumpets and banquets – did you hear?
The everlasting life so near

**…and the spirit returns to God who
gave it. Ecclesiastes 12:7**

# No Worries

Waking with knots of worry
Fear and panic do I hear
Come lift me Lord, please hurry
Bring the peace that I hold dear
Loose these knots, fear will scurry
No more strongholds, chains or fear
Healing breeze, words come surely
Awesome presence very near
Past is gone let it bury
You will catch my one last tear
Return on horse of fury
No prison can keep me here!

**Therefore encourage one another with
these words. 1 Thessalonians 4:18**

# One-Eighty

Get away from me
Satan, you must flee
Your allure is now bereft
Your spirits of fear have left
Nothing's as it seems
You can't have my dreams
He whispers when I am low
I have to tell him to go
Just take out the trash
Symptoms, guilt and flash
My Father loves me I know
Truth in His word He will show
All the world will see
How He set us free
Forget all the petty stuff
Jesus is more than enough
Angels' heads will bow
Turn one-eighty now

**Resist the devil and he will flee from you. James 4:7**

# Just Do It

The whole world is falling apart
Lord, I feel it breaking Your heart
We hear this one and that one
'Til we shut out Your dear Son
Need His words in front of our eyes
Holy Spirit clearing the lies
Read it for yourself indeed
As each one of us must heed
Listen to him – don't shut the door
One day you won't hear anymore
You will bow on bended knee
That day – Jesus Christ you'll see
Call upon Him while He is near
Whisper His name and God will hear
Believe it and get a clue
Before it's too late for you
Repent and turn – do it today
Give Him your heart – what do you say?

**"Everyone who calls on the name of Lord
will be saved." Romans 10:13**

# O Israel

O, the horror, my eyes cannot escape
Turn it off, turn it off, where can I go?
Today this world is in terrible shape
Yet, You said it would happen; it is so.
We say we don't live there; it could be here
Disaster, explosions, rumors of war
Help us! In our mind's eye is looming fear
Far away death touches us where we are.
Life interrupted as seen on the news
Claiming the city walls of that choice land
While discussions circle opposing views
The remnant protected by His right hand.
When all fall around you, just hold steady
I hear horses hoof beats, I think I see
Mighty angels standing at the ready
He said watch and pray and focus on Me.

**"And so Israel will be saved…" Romans 11:26**

# Dropped From Society

Speaking scriptures important, It's a matter of life and death,
He said Don't drop the name of Jesus. In this country
I must hear it, I say Is there fear in your silence? Can we
think for ourselves, clicking instead? Letting life happen,
are we? Hoping to get through, living day by day. Turned away
and ignored Him; Stood by while generations did the same.
Stop depending on yourself; Look to Jesus daily, speaking
His name. That is where the power is. You never know, today
He might stop by. Repent before it's too late. Soon all will see
and know the reasons why. Liberty is why He came. You have
rights that can't be taken away. He's provided gifts for you.
Amid courts and those laws misunderstood, The Advocate
pleads your case. Proof of God's love, worthy, worship and
pray. Awarded life after death. Victory to Him who came
to do you good.

**Keep yourselves in God's love as you wait for the mercy of
our Lord Jesus Christ to bring you to eternal life. Jude 1:21**

# Into the New Millennium

Into the new millennium
Keep fear at zero minimum
Many changes and many years
Look how God took away their fears
We're alive, know the enemy
Others believed and so can we
We have knowledge, we've come so far
Know your Master knows who you are
Be sure to tell Him you still care
And speak The Word in loving prayer
Then no matter how you're feeling
Someone somewhere receives healing
Have all; remember, feed the poor
Still hungry souls need love for sure
Time is so short, we must hurry
Love others; no time to worry
Through weary days we'll soon be gone
Aunts and uncles, cousins, hang on
Share good mem'ries a few more years
Eternal banquet, no more tears

**He who was seated on the throne said,
"I am making everything new!" Revelation 21:5**

# *Yes, There is Hope*

I heard a child say, "There's no hope."
God made a way for us to cope
Precious, just listen to your heart
Jesus already took your part
We'll pray for you until the end
And hope and light in Him we send
Take Him into your heart and know
Love and peace wherever you go
There is hope in His Spirit life
Just don't listen to all the strife
Your hope is heaven, God would say
No one can take that hope away

**In his great mercy he has given us new birth into a living
hope through the resurrection of Jesus Christ...1 Peter 1:3**

# Good Morning, Lord

Thank you for waking me
Up today. I hardly know what to say.
You made a way on Crucifixion Day for me to pray,
and I will say that I will do that today. I hear my spirit say,
'Wake p and pray. You can do it today.'
I have all manner of prayers today.
I have His authority to say,
'Go and pray. Use caution and pray. Stop and pray.'
Hear me today. I AM is the way.
Your Son has rescued today the helpless along the way.
Flooding at bay. Tempters will pay. Forgive them and pray.
Hear what I say. From beginning and today.
He has heard all who pray. What does the Bible say?
Cease not to pray. See differently today.
Give it all up and pray. Release it today.
Throw trouble His way.
Enough faith for today. Jesus made a way.
I love you I say. We'll just sing and pray.

**Come now, and let us reason together. Isaiah 1:18**

## Hurricane Survivors

HUGO YOU GO – WE WILL BE BACK
No plan seems to take the right tack
Windows boarded and sandbags stacked
Pray Charleston will stand getting whacked
What's the latest from the storm trackers?
Where can we go in the rain, hackers?
Already too late
Can't evacuate
Batteries, candles, water and bread
Waiting. . .waiting, hide feelings of dread
Locomotive sound
Circles east around
Terrifying doughnut overhead
Silent eye center, thick, black and dead
"Come back in here now!"
Inland sweep somehow
Neighbors with flashlights down the street
Sing and pray while the west winds beat
More black nights ahead in this heat
Lay down on the floor, dogs at your feet
Try to go to sleep
Lord, our souls do keep
Please protect the church and all our friends

Bring us through the night when this storm ends
I am not afraid
Promises You made
Are y'all okay? Is that morning light?
Yes, we made it but oh, what a night!
Come outside and see
Pieces of debris
Can you believe this devastation?
No bath, cooking, phones, more frustration
Stormed inland for miles
Timber down in piles
Picked up tornados on the way
As far as Ohio they say
Lick, lick, lick, storm came through this room
There's many thought they'd met their doom
Get the camp stove out
We're okay – no doubt
Hurricane Hugo was not my first
Hazel, Diane but this was the worst
Gotta cook the meat
Outside help is sweet
Most landmarks, signs and power lines down
Trees on their cars, they can't get to town
Pray for others too
Lots of work to do
Everything's moved, animals are gone
It's been a week – the power's on!

**Have no fear of sudden disaster. Proverbs 3:25**

# Our Rescuer

With courage, He walked through the rubble
Overwhelming wood, hay and stubble
In darkness, He reached out His right hand
Encouraging us to take a stand
He came to rescue others, too
He died for me, He died for you
He lives again
To rescue men
Tireless devotion, reaching again
To save as many lives as He can
Forget the sin
Just look for Him

**...our refuge and strength, an ever-
present help in trouble. Psalm 46:1**

# The Real Hero

Football heroes we can claim from our high school days
Local teams, national fame we watch all their plays
Firefighters and police, rescue teams all heroes in disaster
Doctors, equipment ready; it seems dogs making the find faster
Even actors, guardsmen too, heroes from each war
Pioneers, presidents knew courage carries far
Fathers and mothers giving their all, volunteers show, preachers teach
The real hero, Jesus, when we fall, He's looking for hands that reach
His love can rescue mankind, airlifts to safe place
Look toward heaven and find Hero's smiling face

**I see four men in the fire...and the fourth is
like the Son of God. Daniel 3:25 (KJV)**

## Another Blizzard

Started that night big fluffy flakes
An inch an hour for goodness sakes
Flip the channels, see what they say
Still snowing?…still snowing…all day
White-out this morning, blizzard…yes
Christmas travel plans changed, I guess
Disappointment for some, that's true
Stranded…Father, what can I do?
Pray for their safety, pray right now
Tow trucks to rescue, skilled know how
Keep desperate shoppers from harm
Hide the homeless and keep them warm
Cars are covered roof to hood
We still have power, life is good
Twenty-two inches, record snow
Other blizzards long ago
Christmas week the Babe is born
We'll be ready, exciting morn
Beautiful flakes from here inside
Let the plows roll on, we'll just hide

Back to back blizzards 2010
Twenty inches, twenty again
Cabin fever after a while
Refreshment will bring back your smile

**"Do not let your hearts be troubled and
do not be afraid". John 14:27**

# Our Great Nation

It's not about me
We want to stay free
We'll get through this – we
Spirit all can see

Those who are left behind
Know this, God will be kind
Serving, we want to give
For as long as we live

Living on this shore
We've seen fear before
Differences galore
Let evil no more

Block our freedom's pathway
Yet, be that as it may
Americans we pray
Will stand another day

So, let our flags be unfurled
Before all the watching world
Remember, faith sees you through
God Bless America, too

**You are the light of the world. Matthew 5:14a**

# DC Diamond

Right around the corner from the world
Underneath our flag that is unfurled
Our country's White House belongs to all
Where we can still pray and send the call

CHORUS:
Right around the corner from the world
There's a diamond in DC
Capital for all to see
Protected democracy
Freedom land for you and me
Right around the corner from the world
Right around the corner from the world

City order by mounted police
Monuments and churches offer peace
Neighbors of our National Archives
We will carry laws that change our lives

Right around the corner from the world
First ladies' dresses and batons twirled
We will serve this nation tried and true
Mr. President, we honor you

**A city that is set on a hill cannot be hidden. Matthew 5:14b**

# Texas

Loyal men wear boots
Royal western suits
Horses not tied up outside; it's a pickup or car
Cadillac, cowboy no longer a lone star
He may be a cop or a preacher
Talkin' Holy Ghost and the Teacher
His wife shops the four-decker mall
She walks beside him, heard his call
Strong women, turquoise earrings, stud shirt
Denim vest, rings, rings, soft boots, long skirt
Si, Esperanza
Extravaganza
We'll have chili con queso, fajitas, please
Dr. Pepper, taco salad, more of these
Mesquite ribs, pecan pie for you?
Cotton-pickin' raised in Plainview
Thought I saw an armadillo
Cross the road in Amarillo
I might not make it to Laredo
But I saw Ft. Worth and Salado
A house near Dallas
More than a palace
San Antonio, Alamo, Riverwalk

All kinds of Music, people, all kinds of talk
Country western and Mexican guitar
Acres of sky everywhere we are
Oh, look! Flowers – blue, red, yellow
Rodeo cowboys, calves bellow
Hot food, come one, come all
Don't Mess With Texas, Y'all

**Nevertheless, the solid foundation of
God stands, 2 Timothy 2:13**

# Charleston

It's been said, a national test
South Carolina is the best
Vacation spot east coast to west
Flowers and weather beat the rest
Southern Living, I saw it too
Charleston's battery loved it, true
Plantations, hist'ry, southern view
Palmetto, moon, flag bonnie blue
April the ultimate celebration
Dogwood, hyacinth, heady sensation
Showy azaleas bring transformation
Top to bottom blooms the exclamation
Precious magnolias, church and southern belles
Camellias, gardenias, baskets, seashells
"We take care of our own" radio tells
Hurricane warnings, beaches, ocean swells
Trees and houses fell hard that year
Life's not so gentle now I fear
Some mem'ries always bring a tear

Soft words like roses I still hear
Rainbow Row and horse carts I see
Wisteria, Spanish moss blows free
'Que, fish or s'rimp tonight for me
April, return, Charleston's cape be

**God saw all that he had made, and it
was very good. Genesis 1:31**

# Springtime

Wake up! Wake up! It's Springtime!
Curtains fluttering again
Smell the roses, take the time
Cold months away, until then,
Enjoy the bright, warm sunshine.
Hear the mourning dove and wren
Geese flying in a V-line
Fly north, somehow they know when.
Look! Dogwood! That's a good sign
Daffodils blooming again
Lilacs, roses just behind
Lovely petals fall and blend.
Ssshhh! Make them stay in my mind
Barely breathing, season's end
Shattering sounds, engines whine
Cooking, laughing, more to send
Bringing boaters, fishing line.
In the morning I'll pretend
While it's peaceful and sublime
It's Sringtime once again!

**This is the day the Lord has made; Psalm 118:24**

# Brilliant Colors

Brilliant colors pop up and shine
Every other tree is on fire
Keep your eyes on the road, driver
Quick glances capture the minds desire
Each trip more colors turned from green
Don't miss their full peak here or there
Harvested cornstalks, shades of mums
And rows of pumpkins everywhere
Rusty red and golden orange
Air alive with what lies ahead
Shades of green like you've never seen
Skip Halloween, Harvest instead
Roast pork, cranberries, turkey, see?
Warm meals, consider the bounty
Faster pace to get here and there
Colors into the next county
Capture them, paint them, if you can
No picture shows the colors true
Remembering these ooohhs and aaahhs
Be surprised again next year, too

**Celebrate the Feast of Ingathering Exodus 23:16**

# Christmas Eve

There was no snow on that Holy Night
Palm trees swaying and a strange new sight
The bright star shining high in the east
No fear, no lowing or bleating beast
For that rapt moment only a hush
The sound of angels' wings as a rush
Glad new singing, The Child has been born!
A King, a Savior, that early morn
Compelling all to follow that star
The gospel reaching those near and far
A sense of peace that all would be well
Each year over the story would tell
All those who seek bringing gifts of love
Knowing the Babe was sent from above
Gifts were given yet none that we see
Hope and joy freely given to me
Awaiting the next news angels bring
And think of Jesus when the bells ring
I will listen while the stars shine bright
This year again on Christmas Eve night

**...and she gave birth to her firstborn son, Luke 2:7**

# One Night of Peace

It's that time of year again
Cards from folks since way back when
So many hurting and some have nothing to give
This year many are gone. . .we need Christmas to live
Help me get up. . .one. . .two. . .three
I can give a part of me
I want to hear the music; look at all the lights!
Christmas programs, peaceful songs, decorated sights
Cards and gifts are wrapped and sent
Consider. . . all. . .that. . .eve. . .meant
Anticipation, palm trees and a donkey ride
God had a plan for Mary; Joseph by her side. . .
They saw His star in the east
Awed by The Child; man, and beast
Visits, turkey dinner, the American way
Peace waiting – I love You, Jesus – it's Christmas Day!

**Glory to God in the highest, and on earth
peace, good will toward men. Luke 2:14**

# That Christmas

Under midnight blue skies of Morocco one night
Waving palm trees, a warm breeze and sheep bells
I felt like Mary and the scenery right
Closer to the story the Bible tells
I too had a baby boy just two months old then
That year's focus, I pondered the story
A mother, a son, pondered again and again
Did other sons bring the gift of glory?
Thoughts of the journey, the payment, far from hometown
Stable animals, the laws of the Jews
Everything changed the night the guiding star shone down
Available to all was the good news
He came down from heaven to a stable lowly
Not to a palace or a kingdom here
Our belief and understanding dawn so slowly
With Jesus on earth, God was very near
Mary treasured a few years with her Precious One
With hand's work and God's work, children soon fly
When did she know she had seen the face of God's Son?

Mothers, this is but a fleeting goodbye
By faith we believe the story, hear every part
Trusting God as he molds and shapes His men
Love will survive fear, Mary pondered in her heart
Love surrounds us when Christmas comes again

**...a Savior has been born to you; he is
Christ the Lord." Luke 2:11**

# *New Year One*

We opened all those boxes
Guarded the little foxes
Cards, visits, meals, phone calls made
Greetings, love and meaning bade
We watched Big Apple drop the ball
No desire to be there at all
In all that crowd out in the cold.
Too much fun; guess I'm getting old
Well, there is one thing that I do miss
It's having someone special to kiss
This is it…there goes another year
All ahead His promise, have no fear
Year and millennium end
Gone, too late to change and mend
At this moment all in free
History what was to be
Now the computer shows it's true
Turn over new calendar too
Oh one…oh one…oh one…it's here!
New century! Happy New Year!

**In the year of Our Lord January 01, 2001**

# Waking

Thank You, Jesus, when I wake at dawn,
You make me smile for Your sake.
Unsure I seem before the light beam…
was it just a dream?
Where have they gone? Am I living on?
Oh, look…it's the light of dawn!
I hear You say I need to pray,
and I know You're the only way.
Come show me how I can serve
You now and fulfill my premium vow.
Take my hand in Your right hand and secure the band of honor.
Protect me today and all I say and please forgive my delay.
Thank You, I'm intact, don't let the devil distract,
for we have a covenant pact.
I believe all is well, I know I fell,
but of Your mercy I will tell.
I hear the sound of Your sweet voice and I'm not on the ground,
for the heaven train I am bound.
Don't leave me behind, I love You so,

and I want the world to know,

we can all go and beat the foe…

O, praise Your holy name! I heard the call to go and tell all of Your grace

before wrath is served.

We turn to You now in love, we seek reunion above, t

he bride and the dove, and look for the face of the Father.

I pray in Your name, this day is not the same

and You will show them why You came.

**I wait for the Lord…and in his word
do I hope. Psalm 130:5**

# Shame

Jesus came and took my shame of that I have no doubt.

It's not a game, gave up the blame and I am not the same.

The only thing that matters is that name.

No excuse, I am of use, so stop the abuse of nightmares and pain.

My Savior loves me don't you see, so memory leave me be.

The past is past; I'm free at last, no more denial or sin blast.

Though life is mean, I'm still washed clean and my sins cannot be seen.

I'll lose the weight, it's not too late and He is my soulmate.

O, happy day when I heard You say that Jesus is the way.

He took my guilt and my faith is built on the Rock, the Cornerstone.

O Rejoice with me for I'm still free and together we may live to see the return of The charger and Light. I

t will be a life dream for me to see our heavenly garden.

Drifting over streets of gold, singing as He meets men of old and all who were given pardon.

He wrote in the sand and it was grand and by faith I still believe.

**For he will abundantly pardon. Isaiah 55:7**

## Attention!

All those who, would listen to,
God's point of view today.
He sent His Son, and what have we done?
Spoken to none?
Look what He did for you.
Many have lied, but you know that He died,
and you can run but you can't hide.
A WARNING: someday you will bow,
might as well do it now,
He can show you how, to live the best life.
Jesus was the Man and the King,
trusting Him your spirit takes wing,
His praises and worship you'll sing.
I pray over you to convert,
forget about a mountain of hurt,
and rise up out of the dirt.
Confess of your need and your sin, t
he Father wants you to win,
and through that gate you'll go in.
O God, raise them up to forgiveness and love,

I want them to meet with The Dove, and live in eternity above.
I want to intercede, for I know You love them indeed,
let my prayer be a seed,
in the name of Jesus and for His sake.
Agreed.

**Believe on the Lord Jesus Christ, Acts 16:31**

# Remember the things of the Lord

Remember the things of the Lord you read
What He has done for me, He'll do for you
His promises are true; don't be misled
When you see the light, you'll know what to do
Punishment without Him, not by His hand
When you choose Him, your life is not your own
Jesus paid the price for His promised land
The seed must die before life can be shown
Territory of your heart is His claim
His life your promise to creation new
Speak out assurance; remember His name
By faith trust the Bible, it's truth for you
But refuse God's gift and all see His wrath
Victory over sin and peace your bliss
Once in a while we all stray from the path
Heaven's promise waiting, remember this.

**Blessed be the Lord, Psalm 68:19**

# I Will Pray

You made a way where there was no way
until today for me to pray. What did You say?
That I may stop and pray today? Anytime today?
Okay, I will pray. Sing and pray. Praise to You
and pray. What will they say? Doesn't matter,
anyway. Keep fear at bay. Hear what I say.
Hear what I don't say. You know anyway.
I worship and pray. Soon they will say,
that they will pray. Jesus said to pray every day.
Don't go away from the table today, until you
pray. We want to hear well done today.
Wake up each day and vow to say, "I will pray."

**My sheep hear my voice, John 10:27**

# And...

There I was, full of worry, struggling to understand and...
butting my head against a wall of sin and nightmares
from the past. I kept asking myself what else I could
possibly do to find direction, achieve peace and...
You showed Your mercy. You listened while I was
wandering through good enough and it'll be all right
until I looked back and saw all the terrible things I had
covered up. I repented and You turned the key to unlock
my prison of false guilt. My past no longer had control
over my future. I walked away, right out into the light
of spiritual freedom. I'm free and...?
Continue in my Word, pray, use the gifts I gave you.
I am happy for you and delighted with you and I enjoy
our time together, You said, and I will show you new
songs and new ideas. Your love is powerful, Lord,
I can feel the excitement of new things ahead and...!

**There remains, then, a Sabbath-rest for
the people of God;... Hebrews 4:9**

# The Grace of God

Grace Grace Grace we live in the age of Grace
God's Grace toward us no matter what we face
As bad as it looks the worst is held back
Temptation will be there; put down your pack
Take His Grace, available; take it now
Before we're destroyed, make amends, avow
What keeps me in line with no thought of sin
Speaking by faith I have God's Grace within
Don't throw mud on a princess in your keep
Don't give away pearls of wisdom so cheap
There are so many words still left unsaid
Please, let's say them all before long we dread
The Gift and Goal is God's Mercy and Grace
Live on that 'til we see Him face to face.

**Grace and peace to you from God our Father and
from the Lord Jesus Christ. Romans 1:7**

# Stopwatch Running

Jesus has increased the pace
Continue to run the race
Time is compressed, don't you know?
It will soon be time to go
Tell your faith to quickly grow
Get on board, now don't be slow
You know your work, I know mine
Singers, go to the front line
Rider coming; that's your sign
Much to do before we dine
Urgent messages He knows
Every moment Spirit flows
Watch and pray, the rooster crows
Ready? Soon the trumpet blows
Visions will be made quite clear
You don't want to be left here

**So, you also must be ready, because the
Son of Man will come at an hour when you
do not expect him. Matthew 24:44**

# *Time To Love*

In these days of rumors, war and fear,
A new beginning and a new year;
America must turn a new leaf,
Put aside all ignorance and grief.
Nothing matters much anymore,
But knowing what we're put here for;
To worship our Lord and to love,
As faithful as the turtledove.
Our world is growing very small;
Time for sharing God's love for all.
Communication wins the fight;
Battles in prayer and in His might.
We can trust in Him, His words are true;
Rest assured He will come for us - view.
Love so amazing, faith believes so,
And someday all the people will know.

**How great the love is the Father has**
**lavished on us... 1John 3:1**

## Taken Up

You've taken up His Word, my friend
Now, so much more you'll comprehend
Chosen obedience assumed
By the refining fire consumed
Imitate Him – picture this
He will greet you with a kiss
Warmth and joy unmeasured day
He'll say, Rise up, come away
Prepare for travel night or noon
We'll be taken up with Him soon
Follow His lead, lighter than air
Instant understanding up there
Through the Gate, the Light of dawn
He will take us further on
Stand before the Father King
Receive honor, robe and ring

**And this is what he promised us-
even eternal life. 1 John 2:25**

## Leaving Town

Well, I'm moving again
Sure I heard someone call
Winds of change, no fear then
Sorted, good order all
This chance is mine
It'll be fine
When you see me again
We'll be above it all
Together in heaven
Because we heard Him call
Freedom from time
Vision sublime
We'll never move again
Because He heard the call
What a life this has been
His gift was worth it all
Spirit, oil, wine
Come, let us dine!

**After this I looked, and, behold, a door was
opened in heaven... Revelation 4:1**

## Hope of Heaven

Looking forward not looking back
Not focusing on pain or lack
Repentance has changed my hindsight
Turning toward that warm bright Light
The Chosen One Who died for me
Opened the way that I could see
His provision for all my needs
Moved my giving and planting seeds
Motives for all the right reasons
Thanking Him for many seasons
Some thought He would come before this
That's one call I don't want to miss
Stronger now and no debating
Resting inside while I'm waiting
To hear Him say that I've done well
Notice heaven's sweet fragrant smell
Anticipation since we met
Lavish banquet table all set
Abundant excellence to share
Forever joyful life up there

**Now may the God of hope fill you
with all joy...Romans 15:13**

New Beginning

Printed in the United States
By Bookmasters